HERCULES

D0622650

# Politics and Government in Ancient Rome

Daniel C. Gedacht

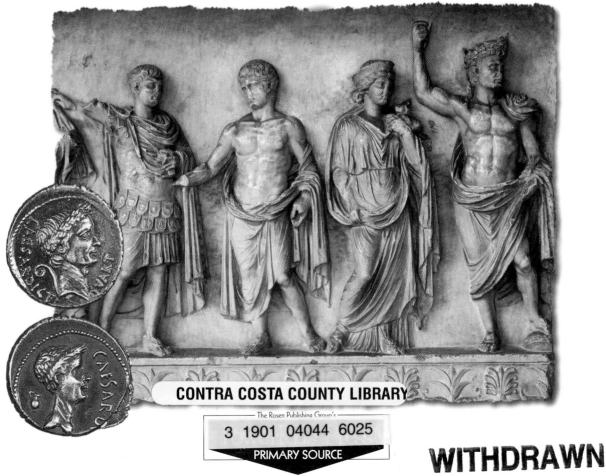

CONTRA COSTA COUNTY LIBRARY

3 1901 04044 6025

WITHDRAWN

The Rosen Publishing Group's

PRIMARY SOURCE

New York

*For Julie, Mike, and especially Alex*

Published in 2004 by The Rosen Publishing Group, Inc.
29 East 21st Street, New York, NY 10010

Copyright © 2004 by The Rosen Publishing Group, Inc.

All rights reserved. No part of this book may be reproduced in any form without permission in writing from the publisher, except by a reviewer.

First Edition

Editor: Rachel O'Connor
Designer: Michael J. Caroleo
Photo Researcher: Adriana Skura

Photo Credits: Cover and pp. 7, 15 © Scala/Art Resource, NY; cover (inset) © Snark/Art Resource, NY; p. 4 © Giraudon/Art Resource, NY; p. 8 Galleria Degli Uffizi, Florence, Italy/Bridgeman Art Library; pp. 11, 20 (inset) The Art Archive/Museo della Civita Romana Rome/Dagli Orti; pp. 12, 19 The Granger Collection, New York; p. 16 (statue) The Art Archive/National Museum Bucharest; © Stock Montage/SuperStock; p. 19 (statue) The Art Archive/Musée du Louvre, Paris/Dagli Orti; p. 20 (statue) The Art Archive/Museo Capitolino Rome/Dagli Orti.

Gedacht, Daniel C.
Politics and government in ancient Rome / Daniel C. Gedacht.— 1st ed.
    v. cm. — (Primary sources of ancient civilizations. Rome)
Includes bibliographical references and index.
Contents: Roman rule—The monarchy—Rome under the monarchy—The early republic—The struggle of the orders—Victories for the plebeians—The Roman military—Imperial rule—After Augustus.
  ISBN 0-8239-6777-8 (library binding) — ISBN 0-8239-8948-8 (pbk.)
1. Rome—Politics and government—Juvenile literature. [1. Rome—Politics and government.] I. Title. II. Series.
  DG83 .G43 2004
  937–dc21
                                                                        2002156301

Manufactured in the United States of America

# Contents

④

# Roman Rule

The government of Rome had three main stages from the time of Rome's beginning in 753 B.C. to the fall of the Roman Empire in the fifth century A.D. The first period is known as the regal period, when Rome was governed by a monarchy. This period lasted about 250 years. Next came the Republican era. This was a time of great conflict both within and outside the empire. It was also a time of great social and political development. The last stage in government in the Roman Empire came with imperial rule. This period began when Augustus became Rome's first emperor in 27 B.C.

◀ *According to Roman mythology, Rome was founded by the brothers Romulus and Remus. After slaying Remus, Romulus became Rome's first king. In this painting, Romulus traces the boundaries of Rome.*

# The Monarchy

It is believed that a series of seven kings governed Rome from the time it was founded until the beginning of the Republic in 509 B.C. As ruler, the king governed Rome with absolute power, or imperium. The king was selected and granted power by the Senate, which was composed of various heads of families. The king was then approved by the Curiate Assembly. All male citizens, men who could prove that both parents were native Romans, were represented in the Assembly. The Senate oversaw the king to make sure that he was ruling according to the unwritten laws and traditions of Rome. The main function of the Assembly was to confirm imperium to the king, who had been selected by the Senate.

*Numa Pompilius* (right), *the legendary second king of Rome, is shown here in this painting with the famous philosopher Socrates* (left). ▶

7

# Rome Under the Monarchy

During the regal period, the Roman military was busy capturing land surrounding the city. As a result, Rome grew in size and power. However, during the sixth century B.C., Rome was captured by the Etruscans. The Etruscans lived north of Rome in Etruria. According to stories passed down over time, Rome was ruled by Etruscan monarchs until Lucius Junius led a revolt in 509 B.C. This revolt forced the Etruscans out of Rome.

Roman society consisted of two main groups. The upper class, or patricians, controlled most of the wealth and power of Rome. The lower class, or plebeians, made up most of society. They were mainly farmers and craftsmen.

◀ *This sixteenth-century painting shows Tarquinius Superbus, the last king of Rome, founding the Temple of Jupiter on Capitol Hill.*

# The Early Republic

The removal of the Etruscans saw the end of regal rule in Rome and the beginning of the Republic. The republican government was set up so that any one individual could not gain too much power. The republican senate consisted of a group of wealthy patricians. This was the only group elected for life. They were very powerful. Two consuls were elected for one-year terms. The consuls had imperium, but each consul could veto the other. Under the consuls were other officers, including two or more finance officers called quaestors, and two or more praetors, or judges. There were three citizen assemblies that voted to elect officials and pass laws.

*This sculpture shows the Roman senate in a procession to honor a consul taking office. Consuls were elected at the beginning of each year.* ▶

# The Struggle of the Orders

Early in the Republic, only people from the patrician class were allowed to be elected consul. Therefore, the patricians held most of the power in Rome. This led to great tension, known as the struggle of the orders, between the patricians and the plebeians. The plebeians were trying to gain social and political equality, while the patricians were trying to maintain the control of Rome. In 471 B.C., the plebeians withdrew from Rome to the Sacred Mount to form an assembly of their own. The decisions of this assembly related only to the plebeians. The patricians found it was hard to run Rome without the plebeians and therefore decided to meet some of their demands.

◀ Top: *This print shows a court scene in ancient Rome. The first Roman code of law was developed during the early Republic.* Bottom: *The forum was the center of Roman business and politics.*

13

# Victories for the Plebeians

In response to the plebeian revolt, the patrician senate established a written legal code. In the past, justice had been based on a judge's personal understanding of the law. The new written code, called the Law of the Twelve Tables, was created in 450 B.C. It was an important first step in gaining equal rights for the plebeians. Another result of the struggle of the orders was that, in 367 B.C., plebeians were allowed the right to be elected consul. The most important victory of all, however, was in 287 B.C. It was decided then that the rulings of the plebeian assembly would apply to all Roman citizens, not just plebeians.

*In ancient Rome, the plebeians had the least power but the greatest numbers. They usually worked as farmers, bakers, builders, or artisans. This painting shows a baker, Paquio Porculo, with his wife.* ▶

This sculpture appears on Trajan's column. Trajan was made emperor in A.D. 98 because he was so successful in his military life. The column was completed in 113 A.D. and shows scenes of his military victories against the Dacians, a people who lived in present-day Romania.

# The Roman Military

The military was important to the growth of Rome. Most patrician families sent their sons to military school for training. Afterward, the young men entered politics. A Roman usually entered the military at 17 and served for up to 20 years.

When Rome was at war and experiencing a crisis, the Senate sometimes gave imperium to one person. This position was called dictator. During most of the Republican period, dictators solved crises and then returned imperium to the government. After several wars, Julius Caesar, a general and statesman, was elected dictator for life in 44 B.C. This event marked the end of the Republic and set the stage for the next ruling era.

◀ *Julius Caesar was a brilliant military leader. He led Rome into many battles and gained great power as a result. This power led to envy among his peers and Caesar was murdered by a group of senators in 44 B.C.*

# Imperial Rule

Under imperial rule, the Senate and Assembly no longer held all the power in Rome. Instead an emperor ruled Rome. Augustus was the first of the Roman emperors. He took power in 31 B.C. The republican tradition of two consuls disappeared under Augustus. The power of Rome went to Augustus alone, although he did value the opinion of the Senate and the Roman people. Augustus was called *princeps*, or "first among equals," and was perhaps the greatest reformer that Rome had seen. During his rule, he gave citizenship to all male Italians, resettled soldiers throughout the empire to spread Roman language and culture, and sponsored many building and art projects.

Top: *This picture of the Roman forum at the height of the empire reflects some of the architectural improvements during the reign of Augustus, who is quoted as saying "I found Rome a city of brick and left it a city of marble."*

*This marble statue, dating from 27 B.C. to A.D. 14, is of Augustus when he was emperor of Rome. It can be seen in the Louvre, a museum in Paris, France.*

This is a marble sculpture of Tiberius Claudius Nero, who became emperor following the death of Augustus in A.D. 14. ▶

# After Augustus

The rulers who followed after Augustus' death in A.D. 14, such as Tiberius, Claudius I, and Nero, showed their power by calling themselves imperator, or emperor. These rulers continued in the tradition of conquering lands for the Roman Empire. They expanded the empire into parts of Germany, eastern Europe, most of Great Britain, and parts of northern Africa. In fact, under imperial Rome, the strength of the military was so important that it sometimes decided who would gain power in Rome. Generals with large, faithful armies would use their forces to become emperor. This system lasted until the fall of the Roman Empire in the fifth century A.D.

*Hadrian was emperor of Rome from A.D. 117 to 138. He was a strong military leader and this sculpture from the arch he had built shows his victorious return from a military battle.*

21

# Legacies of Ancient Rome

Rome produced many great rulers throughout its history, and its traditions have influenced governments today. As far back as the monarchy of early Rome, Romans separated power so that one person would not become too strong. This is like the division of power in many modern-day governments. Also, the Roman senate and the assemblies made up of citizens are early forms of democratic governments that are seen in the U.S. Congress and in parliaments around the world.

The word "republic" comes from the Latin *res publica*, "belonging to the people." Many Romans fought hard to create a government in which the people had a voice. Two thousand years later, this voice lives on in many parts of the world.

# Glossary

**consuls** (KON-sulz)  Very important officials.

**craftsmen** (KRAFTS-men) Workmen who practice certain trades.

**culture** (KUL-chur)  The beliefs, practices, and faiths of a group of people.

**democratic** (deh-muh-KRA-tik)  Having to do with a system in which people choose their leaders.

**development** (dih-VEH-lup-mint)  Growth.

**era** (ER-uh)  A period of time or history.

**expanded** (ek-SPAND-ed)  Spread out, or grew larger.

**imperial** (im-PEER-ee-ul)  Having to do with an empire or an emperor.

**influenced** (IN-floo-ensd)  Had the power to produce an effect on others.

**legacies** (LEH-guh-seez)  Things that have been handed down from other people or things.

**legendary** (LEH-jen-der-ee)  Relating to a story, passed down through the years, that cannot be proven.

**maintain** (mayn-TAYN)  To keep up.

**monarchy** (MAH-nar-kee)  A government run by a king or a queen.

**parliaments** (PAR-lih-mints) The lawmakers of countries.

**regal** (REE-gul)  Having to do with kings and queens.

**revolt** (rih-VOLT)  Fight.

**tension** (TEN-shun)  The uneasiness between groups of people or things.

**traditions** (truh-DIH-shunz)  Ways of doing things that have been passed down over time.

**veto** (VEE-toh)  The power of one branch or department of a government not to authorize laws suggested by another department.

# Index

# Primary Sources

**Cover.** Apotheosis of Emperor Augustus. The Imperial Period (27 B.C.–A.D. 396). Octavian relief. Museo Nazionale, Ravenna, Italy. **Inset.** Julius Caesar. Two coins. From the Republican period (510–27 B.C.). In 44 B.C., Julius Caesar began to issue coins with his portrait on them. This was the first portrait of a Roman to appear on a coin while the person was still alive. The coins show Caesar in the "veristic" style typical of the late Republic, in which experience and wisdom are suggested by an apparently truthful record of the person's advanced age. He is shown with a very long, lined neck, and a high, lined forehead that hints at baldness. He is said to have tried to conceal this baldness with the laurel wreath. **Page 11.** Roman senate in procession for consul taking office. Sarcophagus fragment from Acilia, Italy. 270 A.D. Museo della Civilta Romana. Rome, Italy. **Page 15.** Portrait of Paquio Proculo, the baker, and his wife. Roman fresco from Pompeii. Imperial Period. Museo Archeologico Nazionale in Naples, Italy. **Page 19. Right.** Emperor Augustus. Marble statue from Velletri, Italy. 27 B.C.–A.D.14. Musée du Louvre. Paris, France. **Page 20. Bottom Left.** The return of Hadrian, Roman emperor A.D. 76–138. Bas-relief from the triumphal Hadrian's arch. The arch was built in A.D. 131 as part of a wall separating the old and new cities of Athens. On the side of the arch facing the Acropolis it reads, "This is Athens the former city of Theseus." On the other side is inscribed, "This is the city of Hadrian and not of Theseus." The 60-foot (18 m) arch was made of marble.

# Web Sites

Due to the changing nature of Internet links, PowerKids Press has developed an online list of Web sites related to the subject of this book. This site is updated regularly. Please use this link to access the list:

www.powerkidslinks.com/psaciv/polirom/